MUSIC LAW HANDBOOK

FOR CANADA

VOLUME II

MUSIC LAW HANDBOOK

FOR CANADA

VOLUME II

PAUL SANDERSON
Barrister & Solicitor

Copyright © 2015 Paul Sanderson

All rights reserved. No part of this publication may be reproduced or transmitted in any form or by any means – electronic or mechanical, including photocopying, recording or any information storage and retrieval system – without written permission from the publisher, except by a reviewer who wishes to quote brief passages for inclusion in a review.

The publisher gratefully acknowledges the financial assistance of the Canada Council for the Arts and the Ontario Arts Council.

 Canada Council   Conseil des arts
for the Arts   du Canada

Library and Archives Canada Cataloguing in Publication

Sanderson, Paul, 1954-, author
    Music law handbook for Canada. Volume II / Paul Sanderson, barrister & solicitor.

Includes bibliographical references.

ISBN 978-1-927079-39-3 (paperback)

    1. Musicians--Legal status, laws, etc.--Canada. 2. Music trade--Law and legislation--Canada. 3. Music publishing--Law and legislation--Canada. I. Title.

KE3986.M8S242 2015   343.71'07878   C2015-907075-9
KF4291.S262 2015

Design and Typography: Rolf Busch

Published in 2015 by

Seraphim Editions
54 Bay Street
Woodstock, ON
Canada N4S 3K9

Printed and bound in Canada

To Cassandra and Jesse

Imagine ... Always

The following is general advice only and skilled legal and accounting advice should be sought in any specific situation.

For more detailed information, you can also consult *Musicians and The Law in Canada* by Paul Sanderson, published by Carswell A Division of Thomson Reuters Canada Limited.

TABLE OF CONTENTS

- *9*   Author Profile
- *11*   Intellectual Property Law: An Overview
- *16*   Neighbouring Rights
- *20*   Moral Rights
- *24*   A Guide to Licensing Music
- *32*   How Do I Set Up A Music Publishing Company?
- *36*   Key Recording and Publishing Agreements in the Music Business: An Overview
- *45*   Producer Agreements
- *52*   Management Agreements
- *55*   Ten Commandments
- *58*   Wills

AUTHOR PROFILE

Susan Kelly

Paul Sanderson – entertainment lawyer by day and blues musician by night. "A fixed and focused destination, nothing else would do" describes the determination that ensured Paul would not stray far from his love of the arts when choosing his day job.

Paul is the heart of Sanderson Entertainment Law. He has provided legal services to music and arts law clients concerning their specific contractual and legal matters since 1983. Paul also teaches at the Metalworks Institute of Sound & Music Production, providing education on such areas as Entertainment Agreements, Contractual and Legal Aspects of Live Show Production, and Intellectual Property. He is the author of two groundbreaking legal publications, namely, "Musicians and the Law in Canada", published by Carswell Legal Publications, and "Artist Agreements", a book of contract precedents for visual and multimedia artists, published by CARFAC Ontario.

When not wearing his legal hat, Paul can be found performing with Blue Room, a blues band he formed which performs mostly original music. Blue Room have performed at The Silver Dollar, The Rex and the Beaches Jazz Festival, among other venues, and have been on the bill with artists such as John Hammond, Buddy Guy and BB King. They have recorded and released 4 CDs and their music has obtained airplay on over 40 radio stations worldwide, including the CBC and Q107 in Canada. Paul plays guitar, writes and contributes background vocals to Blue Room.

Paul is also a member of SOCAN, the Scarborough Arts Council, has exhibited his award winning photography in both solo and group shows, and is a published poet, who is a full member of The League of Canadian Poets.

INTELLECTUAL PROPERTY LAW: AN OVERVIEW

1. What Is Intellectual Property?

Intellectual property is the result of a "creation of the mind" – hence, the word "intellectual" to define the nature of this property. Intellectual property is intangible; therefore, unlike real property, such as a house or land, by its very nature one cannot touch or feel it.

2. Why Is It Important?

Intellectual property is integral to artistic ventures of all kinds. For example, the copyrights that one can acquire in music and sound recordings; the rights in one's trade name, which are based on trademark law; patent law rights that protect inventions; copyright protection of computer software as literary works; all of these rights are integral to artistic and entertainment businesses globally and are part of what constitutes intellectual property rights.

3. What Is The Legal Basis For Intellectual Property Rights?

Intellectual property is defined, granted and protected by a body of law known as intellectual property law. As discussed below, the rights to own and exploit intellectual property rights are granted under specific statutory laws.

There are four main statutes relevant to artistic and entertainment industries that constitute a "family" of intellectual property statutes. These statutes are the basis for intellectual property rights that can be acquired. All of these statutes are federal statutes; that is, like the *Criminal Code* which is also a federal statute, they apply nationally throughout Canada.

The four main intellectual property statutes that are relevant are: The *Copyright Act*; the *Trademarks Act*; the *Patents Act*; and the *Industrial Designs Act*.

4. What Do Intellectual Property Rights Protect?

The *Copyright Act* protects the form of expression of works that are recognized and defined in this statute. These works include, for example, literary works, dramatic works and artistic works such as music, books, films, videos, sound recordings, computer programs.

The *Trademarks Act* protects trademarks and trade names that distinguish wares and/or services in the marketplace. Trademarks consist of, among other things, a word, a slogan, a logo, a name or a sound. The *Patents Act* protects inventions, if the invention meets the three legal tests of uniqueness, inventive merit and usefulness.

The *Industrial Designs Act* protects the aesthetic features of an original design. It is not the functional part of a design, but the aesthetic feature that is protected under this statute. For example, the shape of a lamp, or a pattern for wallpaper.

Subject to the statutory limitations under each specific statute, the rights acquired are exclusive.

Note that none of these statutes protects ideas. Ideas are protected under the laws of trade secrets and confidentiality, not intellectual property statutes.

5. How Can You Acquire Intellectual Property Rights?

Copyrights need not be registered under the Copyright Act in order to acquire such rights. However, there are significant reasons why one would choose to register copyright or trademarks.

To acquire copyright, generally, one must create an original work within the meaning of the *Copyright Act*. One can also acquire copyrights by contract, under a license or assignment in writing from the owner of copyright, for example, or under succession law pursuant to a will for example.

To acquire a registered trademark one must meet the requirements of the Trademarks Act. One can also acquire such rights under a license or assignment in writing from the owner of trademark, for example.

Failure to register a patent or an industrial design will result in one being unable to acquire the exclusive rights available if one had registered such rights.

One must apply to register a patent for an invention within one year of public disclosure of the invention. Industrial designs must also be applied for and registered. Such an application must be made within one year of public disclosure of the design. Patents and industrial designs can also be acquired by virtue of a license or assignment, for example.

6. How Long Do The Rights Last?

The term of protection varies under each specific statute:
(a) The general rule is that copyright lasts for life of the author plus 50 years from the last day in the calendar year after the author's death.
(b) The term of protection for trademarks can be perpetual.
(c) Patents last for 20 years from the date of the application for registration of a patent.
(d) Industrial designs last for 10 years from the date of the registration of the industrial design.

7. Conclusion

Society continues to experience rapid growth of intellectual property based wares and services and is being irrevocably transformed by the digital/computer revolution, which is intellectual property based. The Internet alone has irrevocably shaped and continues to contribute to the exponential changes occurring in our society.

Intellectual property rights have had a significant effect on our society. Can you imagine living without having access to the Internet? How about not having a computer? These are only a few examples of intellectual property based products. Think also of the unquantified, but mind-boggling, number of uses, licenses and assignments of intellectual property of each and every nature that are consumed, exploited and utilized every day, globally; then you can start to grasp the scope of the economic value to and impact on society of intellectual property rights.

NEIGHBOURING RIGHTS

I   What Are Neighbouring Rights?

Neighbouring rights consist of:

1. the rights that makers have in sound recordings;
2. the rights that performers have in their performances in sound recordings;
3. the rights broadcasters have in the communication signals they broadcast.

They are granted under the *Copyright Act* and have existed in Canada since 1997.

Items 1 and 2 above are most relevant to performers on and makers of sound recordings. Several of the key aspects of these sets of rights are outlined below.

The rights referenced in Item 2 above are sometimes confused with public performing rights which are part of the musical copyrights acquired by music whether or not it is embodied in a sound recording. However, these two sets of rights are distinct. One constitutes one of the three main components of neighbouring rights – that is, those rights granted to performers in their performances in sound recordings; the other is part of the bundle of rights that constitute musical copyrights.

II Who is a Maker?

In practice makers are primarily record labels who produce sound recordings. This includes artists who operate their own record production companies and record and own their own sound recordings.

III Who is a Performer?

A performer can be any eligible performer whose performance is on a sound recording. Conditions with respect to a performer's eligibility are discussed below in Section VI.

A performer can be either a featured or non-featured performer. For example, a vocalist and instrumentalists such as a guitarist, keyboardist, bassist and drummer on a sound recording could be featured performers. A non-featured performer could be a backup vocalist and/or a backup musician who is not one of the featured performers on a sound recording.

IV What is the "maker's share" and "performer's share"?

The *Copyright Act* provides that 50% of the revenue collected from neighbouring rights is to be paid to both makers of and performers on sound recordings. This division of revenue constitutes the "maker's share" and "performer's share" of neighbouring rights revenue.

V Why Are Neighbouring Rights Important?

Neighbouring rights can be a significant source of revenue for makers of sound recordings and performers whose performances are embodied in sound recordings. In addition, the *Copyright Act* affords substantial rights to makers and performers.

VI Eligibility To Acquire Neighbouring Rights

There are a number of conditions that must be met by makers and performers to be entitled to payment of neighbouring rights remuneration. The list below is not exhaustive. Consult the *Copyright Act* for more details as to the applicable conditions that need to be met by performers and makers in order to be eligible.

Conditions for eligibility include: whether the performances have taken place in Canada, or a country that has signed the Rome Convention, which is a specific required copyright Treaty, (Rome Convention country) or are fixed (i.e. put in a material form of expression such as a recording) by a Canadian citizen, permanent resident or corporation headquartered in Canada or a Rome Convention country; or are first published in Canada or a Rome Convention country; or, if live, are transmitted by broadcast signal from Canada or a Rome Convention country by a broadcaster having its headquarters in the country of broadcast.

Note – both studio and live sound recordings can be eligible for payment of neighbouring rights remuneration.

VII Who Administers Neighbouring Rights?

Re: Sound is the copyright collective which collects and pays both the maker's and performer's share of neighbouring rights. However, performers and makers cannot join Re: Sound directly. Re: Sound requires eligible performers to join either RACS, MROC or Artisti and eligible makers to join Connect Music Licensing in order for it to be entitled to administer their share of neighbouring rights royalties. Therefore, if an artist is both a performer on a sound recording and the maker of a sound recording, whether or not it is the same recording on which the artist/performer's performance is embodied, then in order to be paid both the performer's and maker's shares of neighbouring rights revenue to which the artist is entitled, the artist needs to join, as indicated above: 1. one of either RACS, MROC or Artisti as a performer; <u>and</u> 2. Connect Music Licensing as a maker. Consult www.resound.ca, RACS, MROC and Aristi websites for more details.

MORAL RIGHTS

I What are Moral Rights?

Moral rights are typically not as well understood or discussed as much as copyrights. This is presumably because copyrights are economic rights and, as such, financial benefits can accrue from exploiting such rights. In contrast, moral rights are non-economic rights. However, this does not mean that moral rights are not significant and there can be serious financial implications if they are infringed.

Moral rights consist of two main rights: paternity and integrity. The paternity right is the right to claim authorship of a work under one's legal name or a pseudonym or the right to remain anonymous. The integrity right applies when a work is distorted, mutilated or otherwise modified, or is used in association with a product, service, cause or institution to the prejudice of the honour or reputation of the author of the work.

Even though they are granted under the *Copyright Act*, moral rights are not copyrights. Moral rights are also distinct from morality issues per se.

II Acquisition

Moral rights are acquired under the *Copyright Act* by authors of copyright protected works. Generally, if a work is entitled to copyright protection, the author of that work is entitled to moral rights. No formalities must be met under the *Copyright Act* in order to acquire moral rights. A work can be any type of work recognized under the Copyright Act. For example, a musical composition or a sound recording would be considered a work. Those who participate in the making of a sound recording, such as recording artists and record producers, acquire moral rights in relation to such works. In addition, moral rights are acquired by performers with respect to their performances in a sound recording.

III Duration

Moral rights subsist for the same term as copyright in a work – that is, life of the author plus 50 years at the end of the calendar year after the author's death. In the case of joint authorship, moral rights subsist for life of the last surviving author of the work plus 50 years at the end of the calendar year after that author's death.

Moral rights, like copyrights, devolve to an author's estate. They can be specifically bequeathed by will, or, in the absence of specific bequest under a will, devolve to the person to whom the copyright is bequeathed. If neither of the above applies, the moral rights devolve to the person entitled to any other property in respect of which the author dies intestate.

IV Practical Issues

Moral rights cannot be assigned, but they can be waived in whole or in part. An assignment of copyright is not a waiver of moral rights.

It is common for one person to own the copyright (a music publisher, for example) and for the original author of the work (i.e. in this case the songwriter) to retain ownership of the moral rights.

An agent can administer moral rights and make decisions regarding their waiver or protection on an author's behalf.

Moral rights issues often arise in the context of music publishing and recording agreements. For example, when a music publisher requests the right to alter or adapt lyrics to a song, or there is a request to use music or a sound recording for advertising purposes, or in X-rated films, commercials, for political or religious purposes, or with respect to certain specified products.

It is common practice in the music industry under such agreements to seek a waiver in their entirety of an author's moral rights concerning musical compositions, sound or audiovisual recordings so that such works can be exploited unfettered by the restraints of moral rights.

Moral rights are also capable of being protected by contract. For example, in situations outlined above, a contractual modification of a full waiver of moral rights may be negotiated. This can ensure that the author is contractually entitled to credit as the author of a work, either under a pseudonym or under the author's legal name, or it can afford the author the right remain anonymous. An author of the music may also, if it is contractually negotiated, be entitled to prevent the use of music or a sound recording in any of the above-noted contexts without the author's prior written consent.

V Protection

The same remedies available for copyright infringement – including an injunction, damages, right to an accounting, profits and delivery up – are available when moral rights are infringed.

The general basis used to assess financial compensation when moral rights are infringed is to assess "damages at large". The courts can also assess punitive damages.

A GUIDE TO LICENSING MUSIC

It is assumed for purposes of this chapter that music licensing rights include copyrights to these three (3) works:

(i) musical compositions;

(ii) sound recordings, which includes the copyright in the sound recordings and the neighbouring right, (that is typically an assignment or a licence) which constitutes consent of the makers of sound recordings;

(iii) performers' rights in their performances in a sound recording.

I. Introduction

a) Generally

What is music licensing? From the legal perspective, it is the right to do an act regarding copyright protected works that only the musical copyright owner can do. From the business perspective it means exploiting copyrights through licensing. Note that a grant of an interest in copyright, (that is typically an assignment or a licence) which constitutes the right to use the copyright must be in writing to be valid under the Copyright Act.

b) Musical Copyrights

There are five main rights and revenue sources:

(i) mechanical rights – that is, the right to reproduce music in a sound recording;

(ii) public performing rights – that is, the right to perform music in public;

(iii) synchronization rights – that is, the right to synchronize music with visual images, such as in film, TV;

(iv) print rights – that is, the right to reproduce music in print form;

(v) subsidiary rights – that is, other rights from which economic value of music may be exploited, such as the rights to alter and translate a work.

II. Administration of Copyrights: The System

1. Generally:

The legal infrastructure of the system is based on the *Copyright Act* and in practice economic value is conveyed by contracts, which are primarily copyright assignments and licenses.

Agreements that are entered into for licensing purposes are non-compulsory. That is, they are entered into on a voluntary basis. Such contracts structure transactions and are the basis of the economic system of how copyright operates in practice.

2. **Main Administrators:**

(a) Copyright Collectives

   (i) Defined

   A collecting society is defined in the *Copyright Act* as an organization engaged by or for those who by virtue of an assignment, licence or by an agency relationship are authorized to act on behalf of their members or affiliates.

   (ii) Functions

   There are two main functions a collecting society must fulfill:

   a) operate a licensing scheme;

   b) collect and distribute royalties.

   (iii) Examples

   The following are examples of copyright collectives:

   a) Reproduction rights organizations such as CMRRA and SODRAC;

   b) Public performing rights society such as SOCAN.

   c) Re: Sound, a neighbouring rights collective.

(b) The Copyright Board

It is a quasi judicial tribunal which is subject to federal court review. It has a statutory mandate under the *Copyright Act*. Generally, its mandate is to set the tarriffs that copyright collectives can charge.

(c) Music Publishers

They are also key administrators of musical copyrights, but they are not copyright collectives. However, they do engage in copyright administration. Music licensing is their main activity.

III. Specific Copyright Licences

(1) Mechanical Licence

a) Generally:

This licence often follows a fairly standard format and is not typically subject to substantial negotiation. It is non-compulsory and non-exclusive.

b) Content:

The contents of a mechanical licence consist of:

1. Grant of rights

The non-exclusive right to reproduce which musical work(s)? There can be limitations on the grant of rights. For example, no right to adapt the music or change lyrics.

2. Territory

These licences are typically restricted to the territory of sale of the recordings made under the licence – for example, the US or Canada.

3. Compensation

In Canada, under the Mechanical Licence Agreement (MLA) an industry negotiated rate applies. This rate is negotiated by the CMRRA on behalf of the Canadian Music Publisher Association (CMPA) for its music publisher members and Music Canada on behalf of record labels.

4. Accounting, Payment and Audit

This is a standard clause in a royalty-based agreement.

5. Revocable

The rights granted can be revocable, if the Licensee fails to pay royalties or if there is bankruptcy of the Licensee, for example.

6. Term

The term is indefinite. It typically lasts as long as royalties are paid.

7. General provisions

These provisions could include a governing law clause which is often added to the agreement.

(2) Synchronization Licence (also customarily referred to as a "Synch" licence)

The provisions of this type of licence are highly negotiable and include the following key issues:

1. Grant of Rights

The grant of rights is non-exclusive and can be for specified media/manner/types of uses and duration.

2. Compensation

A flat fee is the most common form of compensation. However, a flat fee together with royalties may be negotiated, depending on the circumstances.

3. Reservation of Rights

Rights can be granted on a territorial or worldwide basis. "Step up", that is additional payments based on additional media and territories, may be negotiated when additional territories or media uses are required.

4. Credit

This consists of naming the publisher/songwriter and varies based on the media, such as TV/film and industry customs.

5. Irrevocable

The rights granted under this licence are generally irrevocable.

6. General provisions

Such provisions can include:

a. an audit and accounting clause, if applicable;
b. a governing law clause.

7. Term

The term can be specified for a fixed number of years or may be expressed as for "life of copyright" – that is, as long as the copyright lasts.

8. Other

If a worldwide grant of rights is made, then this licence would include a grant of public performing rights for the US from the music publisher as copyright owner.

(3) Master Use Licences

Generally the issues addressed in licences for sound recording masters mirror those in a sync licence.

1. Grant of rights

Typically made on an irrevocable basis, and are non-exclusive.

2. Payment

Often a lump sum and may be negotiated on an MFN basis (most favoured nation basis) compared to other master use and synchronizing rights fees. The master use fee for the master and synchronization fee music are typically considered by industry standards and practice to be equal.

3. Credit

The record label and recording artist are afforded credit.

4. Term

The term can be specified for a fixed number of years, or for life of copyright.

5. ISRC code

This can be obtained from Connect Music Licensing. It is advisable to obtain so that royalties can be tracked.

IV. Musical Theatre Licensing

The rights to place music in a dramatic musical production such as musical theatre are known as grand performance rights or large "P" rights, and are administered by the music publisher directly for a negotiated percentage of gross weekly box office receipts. These licences are not covered by SOCAN which licences the small "p" public performing rights – that is, non-dramatic public performing rights to music.

V. Conclusion: A Few Top Licensing Tips

1) ISRC code – obtain it to track royalties for use of sound recordings.
2) Consider most favoured nations basis licences for synch and master licences.
3) Worldwide synch licences: a grant of rights for public performance of the music is granted by the music publisher, not the performing rights society, for the US territory.
4) Synch and master licenses. They are time-sensitive and highly negotiable. Pre-clear rights if planning on using specific songs and/or recordings, because they are not compulsory and could be denied.
5) "Back end" royalties = public performance rights royalties. This is a material term. Cue sheets should be filed with the relevant performing rights society to ensure such royalties are tracked and paid.

HOW DO I SET UP A MUSIC PUBLISHING COMPANY?

For songwriters who are not able to obtain, or who are not inclined to enter into a publishing agreement with a music publisher, or for those who choose to self-publish their music, "HOW DO I SET UP A MUSIC PUBLISHING COMPANY?" is a highly relevant question.

I. What is required to be a Music Publisher?

Music publishing is the exploitation and administration of musical copyrights. Therefore to be a music publisher, you must acquire musical copyrights. In the case of a songwriter who writes his or her own music, this arises automatically. Musical copyrights are acquired by a songwriter who authors original musical works.

In the case of a music publisher who is not a songwriter and therefore has not acquired musical copyrights by creating his or her own original works, copyrights must be obtained <u>in writing</u>. That is, in order to acquire a grant of an interest in copyright, it must be in writing. This is a requirement of the *Copyright Act*. In practice, musical copyrights are acquired by a music publisher by an assignment (i.e. transfer) of copyrights from a songwriter who has acquired musical copyrights by virtue of writing original music; the assignment is made to the music publisher under a written publishing agreement,.

If you have acquired musical copyrights, you have the potential of being a music publisher. What else is required?

II. Business Names

In order to be legally entitled to carry on business under a name other than your own legal name, "Jane Doe Music Publishing", for example, that name must be registered under the *Business Names Registration Act* in Ontario, or the equivalent statute in any other province in Canada where you carry on business. This typically means that you would register a business name in the province where your head office is situated. If you do not use a business name other than your own name, then registration of a business name is not required.

See *Music Law Handbook* "Business Law 101" chapter for an overview of business entities.

Once the business name is registered (if required), what else is required?

III. GST/HST

If your business earns more than $30,000 gross income, then it is necessary to register for GST/HST. If it does not, then such registration is not required.

IV. What else would be advisable?

a) Socan and other copyright societies

It makes sense for a music publisher to join a performing rights society. SOCAN, Canada's only performing rights society, acquires performing rights of both publishers and songwriters and administers the public performance of musical copyrights in Canada. SOCAN collects revenue from the public performance of music and pays its members their respective share of this revenue. See www.socan.ca for more details. Memberships in other copyright collectives such the CMRRA may also be desirable.

b) Financing

One also might consider the need to acquire financing for one's business. Is a capital contribution to the business by way of a loan or investment necessary or desirable? This may not be required initially.

One can actually set up a music publishing company for very little cost. In fact, the cost of all of the above noted registrations, including GST/HST, SOCAN and business name registrations is quite nominal.

c) Conclusion

Is there anything else that would be advisable?

Yes, a computer, a phone, a desk and, of course, the desire to network in the industry to gain contacts and promote the musical copyrights acquired with a view to exploiting them and earning revenue from such copyrights, which are the main assets of a music publisher's business.

The above is general advice only and skilled legal and accounting advice should be sought in any specific situation.

KEY RECORDING AND PUBLISHING AGREEMENTS IN THE MUSIC BUSINESS:

AN OVERVIEW

Two main types of agreements in two key sectors of the music business – namely, recording and publishing – are discussed below.

I. Recording

Key provisions of five main agreements in the recording sector of the music business; namely:

a) recording / record production;
b) licensing;
c) distribution;
d) master use licences; and
e) 360 deals,

are highlighted below.

a) Recording / Record Production Agreements

1. Artist Obligations:

The artist grants exclusive personal recording services, which include the rights to make audio and audiovisual recordings of the artist's performances and the right to use the name and likeness of the artist (i.e. artist's personality rights) in relation to promoting and selling recordings made under the agreement.

2. Recording / Record Production Company's Rights:

The company acquires exclusive rights to the personal recording services of the artist, assumes all financial risks and owns all rights to the audio and audiovisual recordings, and is granted the right to use the artist's personality rights to promote and sell recordings of the artist's performances.

3. Term:

The term is typically for one initial album and specified options, often for up to three or more additional albums embodying the artist's recorded performances. The term could be longer or shorter, depending on many factors including the musical genre and the record company's practice.

4. Compensation:

The artist typically receives advances from the company (i.e. a pre-payment of artist's record sales royalties). When all advances are recouped (typically, from artist's record sales royalties) the artist is entitled to be paid record royalties.

"Top line" royalties under recording agreements range from 16% to 20% of PPD (i.e. the purchase price to the dealer, also referred to as wholesale), typically 13-16% of these royalties go to the artist and 3-4% of PPD goes to the producer. Record royalties are subject to adjustments according to the territory of sale, sales formats (such as singles, EPs, albums), pricing and sales plateaus. Licensing royalties are generally split equally between the company and the artist. Note that under record production agreements, typically 50% of net receipts goes to the artist and the record production company, rather than a specified percentage of PPD.

5. The Company's Obligations:

    a. The company pays recording and any video production costs, mechanical royalties for songs on the recordings, advances, artist sales royalties and union payments, as applicable. Advances to the artist can include advances for recording and video production costs and tour support advances, for example.

    b. Promotion and marketing costs are also paid by the company.

    c. Accounting and audit obligations are to be fulfilled by the company.

b) Licensing agreements

1. Rights to the Master Recordings:

Rights to the master recordings are licensed by the Licensor, which owns them. Typically this is the entity which took the financial risk to pay for and produce the master recordings.

The Licensor may be an artist who owns the master recordings or a record company.

Under this agreement, the Licensee acquires exclusive

rights from the Licensor to manufacture, distribute, sell, advertise, perform and broadcast the licensed recordings. Such rights include the rights for a specific master, or an album's worth or catalogue of masters in a specified territory or territories.

2. Term:

Typically the term for delivery is for one album, plus any option(s) granted for further recordings. The right to sell recordings derived from the licensed master recordings then often lasts five to seven years from the delivery of the last album under the agreement, or can be for longer periods.

3. Compensation:

Typical top line royalties are higher than when an artist is directly signed under a recording agreement. Why? The Licensor took the risk of paying for record production costs. Royalties range from 20% of PPD - to 25% of PPD, of which 3-4% typically goes to the record producer. Sometimes, rather than on a royalty basis, the agreement is structured on a 50/50 net receipts basis – that is, 50% of net receipts goes to the Licensee and 50% to Licensor. The amount of the advance to be paid to the Licensor is negotiable.

4. Record Company:

The Licensee pays mechanical and record sales royalties, advances, promotion and marketing costs and, if applicable, union payments. The Licensee is also obligated to provide accountings and allow an audit to verify accounting statements and payments.

c) Distribution Agreements

   1. Rights to the Masters:

   Copyrights remain with the record or record production company and the rights to distribute recordings are granted to a distributor or a record company, such as a third party major record label which distributes the recordings.

   2. Distribution / Record Company's Rights:

   The company acquires exclusive rights in a specified territory or territories – for example, Canada or North America. These rights include the right to distribute and sell and, in many cases, the right to manufacture audio and audiovisual recordings made and paid for by the record or record production company.

   3. Term:

   The agreement typically lasts three to five years.

   4. Compensation:

   Depending how the agreement is structured, a range of 20-30% of PPD or net receipts is retained by the distributor; the balance goes to the owner of the recordings which are being distributed. The record or record production company pays for all recording and video production costs, mechanical royalties, union payments (if applicable), advances to the artist, promotion and marketing costs.

d) Master Use Licences

   1. Under this Licence, the owner of such rights licenses the rights to the masters, on a non-exclusive

basis, typically for film, television and commercial uses.

2. Customarily a lump sum fee is paid. Such amount is shared equally between the applicable record production company or record company and the artist, if the artist is signed under either such agreement, or is retained by the artist directly if the artist is not signed under such an agreement but is the owner and therefore Licensor of such master recordings. The artist's share is applied to recoup unrecouped advances paid to the artist under the recording or record production agreement.

e) Note on 360 deals

There are four main sources of revenue in the music business:

1. recordings (both audio and audiovisual);
2. music publishing – i.e. from musical copyrights;
3. merchandising (including endorsements and sponsorships);
4. live performance and personal appearances.

Agreements that encompass all such rights and revenue sources are often called 360 agreements or multi-rights agreements.

Typically, 360 agreements include a record licence or recording agreement range of royalties; publishing or co-publishing rights and revenue; merchandising and live performance rights and revenue.

The percentage range of merchandise and live performance revenue is often 10-25% of gross or net income, but this can vary based on rights/revenue sources and company practices.

See the foregoing parts of Section I, and Section II below, regarding rights and revenue sources from recording and publishing that might be included in such agreements.

II. MUSIC PUBLISHING

Highlighted below are key provisions of five main types of agreements in the music publishing sector, namely:

    a) co-publishing;

    b) standard (often single-song) agreements;

    c) sub-publishing;

    d) administration;

    e) synchronization licence.

a) Co-publishing

This is the most common type of publishing agreement.

Under this agreement, typically 50% of musical copyrights are retained by the songwriter/co-publisher and 50% is acquired by the administrator/co-publisher.

Net revenue under this agreement is typically divided: 75% to the songwriter/co-publisher; 25% to the administrator/co-publisher. This percentage can vary depending on the various types of musical copyrights and ensuing revenue.

b) Standard agreements

This agreement is sometimes referred to as a "full" publishing agreement. Under this agreement 100% of the copyright is assigned to the publisher by the songwriter, and the publisher and songwriter share 50/50 in net revenue. Such shares of revenue are customarily referred to as the "publishers" and "writer's" share of revenue.

c) Administration agreement

Typically, the only copyright granted to the administrative publisher is the right to exclusively administer the copyrights to a song or catalogue of songs. Administration rights typically include the right to collect monies, issue licences for use of the musical copyrights, register copyrights and, in some cases, to protect the copyright being administered by litigating. Typically 10% to 15% of gross or net income (sometimes a higher or lower percentage) is retained by the administrative publisher for administration services provided.

d) Sub-publishing agreements

These agreements are also often referred to as foreign sub-publishing agreements because they are typically entered into for a specified foreign territory or territories, i.e. a country outside of a domestic territory. The typical sub-publishing fees range from 15% to 25% of the gross income in the territory. The term can range typically from five to seven years.

e) Synchronization licences

These licences are similar to the master use licence, but apply to the synchronization of music, not the sound recording, in visual media such as films, television programs or television commercials. Such licences can be territorially based, or apply on a worldwide basis. The compensation paid thereunder is often for a negotiated lump sum fee.

III. CONCLUSION

The terms, conditions and duration of all the above agreements vary widely depending on the situation and the bargaining power of the respective parties.

These agreements are complex commercial documents. The above does not constitute legal advice. In a specific situation one should obtain skilled legal advice.

Keep in mind: "You don't get what you deserve, you get what you negotiate."

PRODUCER AGREEMENTS

One of the most important components in your musical team is your music producer. Even if you are skilled at producing your own music, engaging a skilled producer could make the difference between a good record and a career-defining great record. Therefore it often makes sense to engage a producer who can enhance your performances, your songs and the sound of your recordings as a recording artist.

I. What do producers do?

In order to have success as a recording artist you must have:
1. great songs to record;
2. great performances of great songs on recordings; and
3. great-sounding recordings.

The challenge and the main objective of a musical producer is to produce the best recordings possible given all the relevant factors, including length of recording time, the artist's limitations and strengths, the studio and the recording budget.

In fact a music producer generally oversees every aspect of a recording, including technical, commercial and artistic aspects of the recording.

Producers' services can include: selecting songs to be recorded; selecting personnel to assist with the technical and the artistic aspects of recording – for example, hiring an audio engineer and session musicians; supervising recording sessions; preparing recording budgets; assisting with the business side of recordings, including all required paperwork; re-recording and in some cases mixing and editing recordings; mastering or supervising the mastering and test pressings of recordings.

Some producers also engage in co-writing with the recording artist and act as an arranger, or assist in musically arranging the musical compositions to be recorded. They may also act as the sound engineer for the recordings. Every producer works differently and has a different style of producing recordings.

II. What is in the producer agreement?

The terms of producer agreements can vary widely, depending on whether the artist is signed to a record label or whether the artist is unsigned and working independently. However, a number of issues are relevant to both types of agreements.

The producer's compensation is typically a combination of: a fee for services rendered on a per recording or per album basis; an advance against the producer's record sales royalties; and, record sales royalties. However, these aspects of these agreements can also vary widely. In cases where the producer is "specing", i.e. speculating by offering studio or the producer's time, or both, then there will be little or no fees upfront payable to the producer. However, in such cases, the producer will likely expect to be paid when there is success generated from the recordings produced by the producer. Such payments often include record sales royalties and perhaps a share of third party advances related to the relevant recordings, music publishing income and /or neighbouring rights income (that is, income paid to a performer for their performances on the recording) if negotiated. Each situation differs depending on the bargaining power of the parties and the relevant facts.

Typical fees for a producer can vary widely depending on whether demos or master sound recordings are recorded, whether a record label is involved, and the respective statures of the producer and artist in the industry. Record royalties in the range of 3% to 4% of PPD (wholesale) are common and are customarily only paid to the producer once the artist has recouped 100% of the recording costs of the recordings produced by producer at the artist's applicable net record royalty rate. When this occurs, the producer is entitled to be paid royalties from record sales. However, given the bargaining power and nature of these agreements one cannot assume this will always be the case. For example, some producers have the bargaining power to insist on their fee being paid in full and to have royalties payable, irrespective recoupment of recording costs and at higher-than-customary royalty rates. Each agreement and each scenario should be reviewed carefully regarding the language and the facts and the relevant bargaining power of the artist and producer.

Sometimes the producer under a spec deal retains the copyright to the recordings until the producer has been paid the producer's fees, in full, before transferring the copyright to the artist. Not all agreements are structured this way. Typically, if the artist is signed to a record label, the artist who engages the producer acquires copyrights from the producer so that copyrights to the recordings can be transferred to the record label which is ultimately paying the recording costs and is entitled to ownership of the copyrights to master sound recordings under the artist's recording agreement. The copyrights granted concerning such recordings are exclusive and apply on a worldwide basis.

Typically, the producer is asked to waive moral rights the producer acquired by being a contributing author to the sound recordings. Consult the Moral Rights chapter of this book for more details regarding moral rights.

Producer agreements most commonly obligate a producer to provide producer services to the artist on a "first priority" basis, not an exclusive basis, although there can be exceptions to this situation, depending on the facts.

When royalties are involved it is advisable to include an accounting and audit clause. However, for various reasons not all agreements require a royalty to be paid to the producer. For example:
1. the producer is new in the field and is working on a flat fee;
2. the producer fees are high enough to justify not paying the producer record sales royalties.

The term of the agreement will be specified typically in terms of the time it takes to record the specified number of recordings under the agreement.

III. Key Negotiable Issues

A number of key issues to be negotiated are outlined below.
1. The producer's credit – what it consists of and where it is placed is one of the key clauses to be negotiated. A producer with some bargaining power has the producer credit consistently placed on the back cover of any physical product such as a CD and, customarily, any other place where the credit would appear – including, typically, in at least half-page or greater trade ads.
2. When is the delivery of the specified recordings to be completed? This means completing all aspects of the recording, including obtaining any copyright clearances required.
3. The producer's fee, percentage of record sales royalty, advance against the producer's royalty, and whether

the producer participates in and therefore is paid from other forms of income (such as song writing and neighbouring rights income) are negotiable.
4. There is often a controlled composition clause in the agreement. This clause seeks to limit the amount of mechanical royalties payable regarding controlled compositions (i.e. musical compositions that the producer has written, owns or controls in whole or in part, that are embodied in the recording) to a pre-negotiated total number of songs on a record and often at a rate equal to three-quarters of the industry standard or industry-negotiated rate otherwise applicable per composition. This is highly relevant if the producer co-writes songs in whole or part with the artist and such co-written songs appear on a record that is commercially released. The artist will typically seek to have the producer bound by the applicable controlled composition clause which binds the artist under the artist's recording agreement: otherwise the artist could be financially affected under the controlled composition clause in the agreement with the record company or licensor of the record. Typically, the producer who co-writes with the artist with respect to songs that appear on the record to be produced seeks not to be subjected to a controlled composition clause, so that the producer can receive full mechanical royalties without reduction under the controlled composition clause.

5. The definition of a recording should be reviewed. It should be broad enough to include audio and audiovisual recordings so that the producer is paid royalties for exploitation of the recordings the producer produced in both audio and audiovisual formats.
6. An over-budget penalty is typically part of the agreement – that is, if the producer, who is responsible for the recording budget, goes over budget by a specified percentage, typically 10% of the gross recording budget, then the producer will be liable to pay such amounts either from the producer's advances or royalties otherwise payable.

Many other clauses can be added to the agreement, including representations and warranties which are similar to those in most recording agreements and the right to use the producer's name and likeness. Consider also inducement letter obligations if the producer is carrying on business under a corporation. This is because a producer agreement is a personal services agreement and only the producer can supply personal services as a producer under the agreement. For this very reason the agreement typically states that there is no right of the producer to assign the producer's rights and obligations under this contract to another producer.

Producer agreements can be complicated. There are many other negotiable issues that can arise. Skilled advice should be sought.

MANAGEMENT AGREEMENTS

I. Generally

Under this agreement a manager provides personal management services – i.e. services for personal and career advice and guidance to an artist.

The manager/artist relationship is based on trust between the parties. The success of this relationship is based on the manager's ability to obtain and work contacts in the music industry, provide valuable advice to the artist, and obtain monetary and contractual commitments, all for the advancement of the artist's career.

Usually this agreement requires a long term commitment – five years or more – and typically applies on a worldwide basis. A manager is often integral to an artist's success.

II. Five Main Negotiable Issues: A Discussion

1. <u>Power of Attorney.</u> The power of attorney granted to the manager gives the manager the legal authority to act on the artist's behalf and bind the artist to third party obligations. This right is often limited in scope – for example, to committing the artist to

agreements in the entertainment industry and to entering into only short term agreements on the artist's behalf.

2. <u>Compensation.</u> Commission rates that apply typically range from 10% to 25% of an artist's gross income in the entertainment field. Twenty percent is typical for experienced managers. Exclusions from commissions are often negotiated. For example, advances that an artist receives under a recording agreement which are applied to the costs of record production or to independent radio promotion, or tour support costs, are often excluded from management commission. A "sunset" clause – i.e. a clause setting out a specified decline of post-term commissions to which the manager is entitled – is often negotiated and set out in the agreement.

3. <u>Key person.</u> This clause grants the right to the artist to terminate the agreement, if the key individual or persons guiding the artist's career are no longer doing so.

4. <u>Management expenses.</u> Often approval of the artist is required in writing before the manager can incur expenses on the artist's behalf. Cumulative periodic (typically monthly) and single monetary expense limits should be stipulated in the agreement.

5. <u>Performance obligation.</u> This clause sets out a manager's obligation to obtain, for example, a recording agreement or a specified amount of income, in a specified time frame – for example, 12-24 months from the start of the agreement. This clause typically allows the artist to terminate the agreement if the manager fails to meet such obligation.

Many more clauses relevant to this agreement can be added. Skilled advice should be sought.

TEN COMMANDMENTS

Top ten "to dos" list from the author of the so-called "bible" of the Canadian music industry - "Musicians and the Law in Canada" and author of "Music Law Handbook for Canada".

1. **"Get it in writing"**. I know this is a cliché, but I'm a lawyer and this really does mean something in practice. Even a simple agreement in writing can be more protective of your rights than an oral arrangement which is often hard to prove. Also, in some instances – a grant of an interest in copyright, for example – must be in writing to be valid.

2. **"Know your rights"**. Yes the music business is complicated and it keeps getting more so, but in this day and age, information is often readily available. You can forearm yourself and with knowledge you can also assist your team, particularly your legal counsel. How? By being able to give informed instructions you can save yourself money on fees. You don't need to be up on all the details – that's up to your counsel and other advisers; but being able to get the big picture and give good instructions to your manager, lawyer and accountant will stand you in good

stead in your career. A well-utilized lawyer, for example, can both make you money by negotiating better deals on your behalf and save you money by helping you avoid costly legal career pitfalls.

3. **"You don't get what you deserve, you get what you negotiate"**. Guess what? Almost everything is negotiable and is a negotiation. For example, even deciding where to go for lunch with a friend can be a negotiation. This one is a truism in law and in life. It is something that you can "take to the bank" and live by. Keep in mind also that whoever controls the agenda wins, at the game of negotiation.

4. **"Trusted advisers are worth the money"** No one can succeed wholly on their own. It takes a team. You need a team you can trust and information on which you can rely. Definitely budget and spend your money wisely, but at the end of the day value must be paid for, whether it be good equipment or professional advice. You get what you pay for. Pay your team what they are worth. It is worth the investment.

5. **"It's always about the money"**. When they say it's about trust, honesty, artistic integrity ... that's when ... it's about the money, because it's always about the money.

6. **"Actions speak louder than words"**. When you are confused, listen to what the other side says, but, most importantly, watch what they do. Pay attention to their actions. They may be confused themselves. Actions are where you get the truest sense of what someone wants or is about.

7. **"Have fun!"** It's the music business. If you didn't want to have fun you could have done something that was more secure, lucrative and much more boring.

8. **"The basics apply"**. Always have. Always will. Great songs. Great performances. Great production. Apply the basics. Always.

9. **"The facts are often 3/4 of the law"**. This one is a quote from the autobiography of the late great Mahatma Gandhi, the leader of India, who was also a lawyer. So who am I to question this? Besides, I've found in practice this quote often affords very good practical insights into legal issues and legal problem-solving. So get the facts.

10. **"Know yourself. Be true to yourself"**. It's been said, ""It takes 30 years to build a reputation and 30 seconds to destroy it." Longevity is about integrity. Stay true to yourself and your vision as an artist and person. That way the success that you do achieve will be meaningful.

WILLS

1. Why You Need a Will

Even if you are single, you should have a will. Everyone should have a will.

Why?

When no will is available:

(a) the estate's assets are frozen and the court winds up the deceased's affairs and pays off his/her debts. The remaining estate is then divided according to a rigid set of rules according to intestacy laws;

(b) no thought is given to the deceased's known wishes or the needs of the potential inheritors;

(c) charitable donations, scholarship awards, gifts, grandchildren, godchildren – none of these will be taken care of;

(d) there are complex legal problems that intestacy can cause for common law spouses and business partners.

2. **How to Make a Will**
   (a) Plan what your estate consists of and how you want it to be divided.
   (b) Choose an executor. An executor is a person or trust company that will carry out your instructions set out in your will, including doing everything from making funeral arrangements to notifying the beneficiaries to applying for Canada Pension Plan Benefits to filing an income tax return.
   (c) Tips:
      (i) Make sure that the individual who happens to be an executor is nearby.
      (ii) Choose someone your age or younger – ideally someone who has money management skills.
      (iii) Choose someone who is absolutely honest and reliable.
      (iv) Do not forget to name contingent executors in case your first choice is unwilling and/or unable to act when the time comes.
      (v) Consider appointing co-executors.
   (d) Don't do it yourself, go to a professional.

3. **Conclusions**
   (a) Make a will.
   (b) Review your will periodically, perhaps once a year, certainly every five years or after a major event that can affect your will, such as marriage or divorce.

(c) Keep a complete up-to-date net worth statement listing everything you own and everything you owe, along with a copy of your will, in a safe place such as a fireproof safety deposit box.

(d) Keep your will up-to-date. Births, deaths, divorces, and business deals may make a will obsolete.

Publication Credits

"Intellectual Property Law: An Overview"
CDJA Newsletter January, 2015

"Key Agreements in the Music Business: An Overview"
- Based on the author's notes for a panel discussion at the first CMAO Conference in September, 2014.
- Published in Canadian Musician, Business Column, Part 1 September/October 2015 (Vol. XXXVII, No. 5) and Part 2 November/December 2015 (Vol. XXVII, No. 6)

"Author Profile" Susan Kelly, Polson Borbonniere Financial Planning Associates Newsletter, 2007

"How Do I Set Up A Music Publishing Company?" Songwriters Magazine 2015/16.

"A Guide to Music Licensing" is based on the author's notes to an address at the Commons Institute via webinar in Toronto, February, 2015

"Ten Commandments" – Music Books Plus Blog Site October, 2014